Donald J. Trump
(b. 1946)

QUOTATIONS

OF

Donald J. Trump

APPLEWOOD BOOKS

ISBN 978-1-55709-067-6

Manufactured in the USA

Donald J. Trump

DONALD JOHN TRUMP was born on June 14, 1946. He grew up in the wealthy neighborhood of Jamaica Estates in Queens, New York City. In 1964 he enrolled at Fordham University, but two years later he transferred to the Wharton School of the University of Pennsylvania, from which he graduated in May 1968 with a bachelor of science in economics.

Trump joined his father's real estate business, the Trump Organization, in 1971. Under his leadership, the company expanded its real estate holdings and ventured into hotels, casinos, and entertainment. Trump married Ivana Marie Zelníčková in 1977, and the couple had three children together: Donald Jr., Ivanka, and Eric. By the 1980s, he had become a prominent figure in the New York City real-estate scene, known for his ambitious projects and self-promotion.

In 1987 Trump published *The Art of the Deal*, which became a best seller and further elevated his public profile. His reputation as a savvy businessman and deal maker grew. In 2004 he began hosting the reality show *The Apprentice*, where he famously uttered his catchphrase, "You're fired!"

Trump married his second wife, Marla Maples; they had one daughter, Tiffany. His third wife is Melania Knauss, a former model from Slovenia. Married in 2005, they have one child together, Barron William Trump.

Trump's entry into politics began with flirtations in the 1990s and early 2000s. In 2015 he announced his candidacy for the presidency as a Republican. Despite facing a crowded field of primary contenders, Trump secured the Republican nomination in 2016.

In the general election, Trump faced Democratic nominee Hillary Clinton. He won a surprising victory, earning 306 electoral votes to Clinton's 227. On January 20, 2017, Donald Trump was inaugurated as the 45th president of the United States.

In 2020 Trump sought reelection but faced a strong challenge from Democrat Joe Biden. Biden won the election with 306 electoral votes to Trump's 232. Trump's refusal to concede and his claims of election fraud culminated in the storming of the US Capitol by his supporters on January 6, 2021, leading to his second impeachment by the House of Representatives.

After leaving office, Trump remained a prominent figure in Republican politics, with many loyal supporters. In November of 2022, he announced his candidacy for a second term as president of the United States.

QUOTATIONS
OF
Donald J. Trump

Somebody with the kind of views that are maybe a little bit unpopular—which may be right but may be unpopular— wouldn't necessarily have a chance of getting elected against somebody with no great brain but a big smile.

—Television interview with Rona Barrett, 1980

I'm not big on compromise. I understand compromise. Sometimes compromise is the right answer, but oftentimes compromise is the equivalent of defeat, and I don't like being defeated.

—*Life* magazine, January 1984

Some people have an ability to negotiate. It's an art you're basically born with. You either have it or you don't.

—*Washington Post*, November 15, 1984

*I*n my life, there are two things I've found
I'm very good at: overcoming obstacles and
motivating good people to do their best work.

—*Trump: The Art of the Deal*, by Donald J. Trump
with Tony Schwartz, 1987

I don't do it for the money. I've got enough,
much more than I'll ever need. I do it to do
it. Deals are my art form. Other people paint
beautifully on canvas or write wonderful
poetry. I like making deals, preferably
big deals. That's how I get my kicks.

—*Trump: The Art of the Deal*, by Donald J. Trump
with Tony Schwartz, 1987

I wasn't satisfied just to earn a good living.
I was looking to make a statement.

—*Trump: The Art of the Deal*, by Donald J. Trump
with Tony Schwartz, 1987

*T*he final key to the way I promote is bravado. I play to people's fantasies. People may not always think big themselves, but they can still get very excited by those who do. That's why a little hyperbole never hurts.

—*Trump: The Art of the Deal*, by Donald J. Trump
with Tony Schwartz, 1987

*I*f you don't deliver the goods,
people will eventually catch on.

—*Trump: The Art of the Deal*, by Donald J. Trump
with Tony Schwartz, 1987

*I*n my life, there are two things I've found
I'm very good at: overcoming obstacles and
motivating good people to do their best work.

—*Trump: The Art of the Deal*, by Donald J. Trump
with Tony Schwartz, 1987

I want five children, like in my own family,
because with five, then I will know that one
will be guaranteed to turn out like me.

—*Vanity Fair*, September 1, 1990

*W*hen the students poured into
Tiananmen Square, the Chinese
government almost blew it. Then they
were vicious, they were horrible, but
they put it down with strength. That
shows you the power of strength.

—*Playboy* magazine, March 1990

*W*hat separates the winners
from the losers is how a person
reacts to each new twist of fate.

—*Trump: Surviving at the Top*, by Donald J. Trump
and Charles Leerhsen, 1990

I'm conservative, and even very conservative. But I'm quite liberal and getting much more liberal on health care and other things. I really say: What's the purpose of a country if you're not going to have defense and health care?

—CNN, October 1999

I surround myself with the best people.

—CNBC, November 26, 1999

I came from a home—you know, it's not like some of my friends, they get divorced, but their parents were divorced twice or three times. I came from a home where marriage was just incredible. I mean, my parents truly loved each other.

—*Good Morning America*, December 2, 1999

*P*eople want me to [run for president]
all the time...I don't like it. Can you
imagine how controversial I'd be?

—*Hardball with Chris Matthews*, July 12, 1999

I judge people based on their
capability, honesty, and merit.

—*The Advocate*, February 15, 2000

*I*t's very possible that I could be the
first presidential candidate to run and
make money on it.

—*Fortune* magazine, April 3, 2000

I think the regulations are very tough, but I think they could be made tougher. And where they really have to be made tougher is when somebody is proven to be dishonest, not a mistake, not an honest mistake because look, people make bad business deals all the time. When somebody is proven to be dishonest, really harsh punishment has to take place.

—*Hardball with Chris Matthews*, July 15, 2002

I love beautiful women, and beautiful women love me. It has to be both ways.

—Interview with Fredrik Skavlan, November 2003

*G*et going. Move forward. Aim high. Plan for a takeoff. Don't just sit on the runway and hope someone will come along and push the airplane. It simply won't happen.

Change your attitude and gain some altitude. Believe me, you'll love it up here.

—*Trump: How to Get Rich*, by Donald J. Trump
with Meredith McIver, 2004

*Y*ou're fired!

—*The Apprentice*, 2004–2017

*W*atch, listen, and learn. You can't know it all yourself—anyone who thinks that they do is destined for mediocrity.

—*Trump–The Way to the Top: The Best Business Advice
I Ever Received*, by Donald Trump, 2004

*I*n many cases, I probably identify more as Democrat. It just seems that the economy does better under the Democrats than the Republicans. Now, it shouldn't be that way. But if you go back, I mean it just seems that the economy does better under the Democrats.

—CNN, Wolf Blitzer, 2004

*I*n business—every business—the bottom line is understanding the process. If you don't understand the process, you'll never reap the rewards of the process.

—*Trump: How to Get Rich*, by Donald J. Trump with Meredith McIver, 2004

Since I love what I do, I do it vigorously
and I do it better. Because I inject
it with enthusiasm and passion, it
doesn't feel like work. My passion
spills over to everyone around me and
motivates them to do their very best.

—*Trump 101: The Way to Success*, by Donald J. Trump
with Meredith McIver, 2007

Part of the beauty of me is that I am very rich.

—*Good Morning America*, March 17, 2011

I know the Chinese. I've made a
lot of money with the Chinese. I
understand the Chinese mind.

—*Los Angeles Times*, August 24, 2015

I'm a very compassionate person (with a very high IQ) with strong common sense.

—Twitter, April 21, 2013

I keep asking, how long will we go on defending South Korea from North Korea without payment? South Korea is a very very rich country. They're rich because of us. They sell us televisions, they sell us cars. They sell us everything. They are making a fortune.

—"From the Desk of Donald Trump: South Korea,"
YouTube, April 10, 2013

*L*eadership: whatever happens, you're responsible. If it doesn't happen, you're responsible.

—Twitter, November 8, 2013

17

I will build a great, great wall on our southern border, and I will have Mexico pay for that wall.

—Presidential campaign launch rally, June 15, 2015

*O*ur country is in serious trouble. We don't have victories anymore. We used to have victories, but we don't have them. When was the last time anybody saw us beating, let's say, China in a trade deal? They kill us. I beat China all the time. All the time. When did we beat Japan at anything? They send their cars over by the millions, and what do we do?...They beat us all the time. When do we beat Mexico at the border? They're laughing at us, at our stupidity. And now they are beating us economically.... The US has become a dumping ground for everybody else's problems.

—Presidential bid announcement, June 16, 2015

*O*ur enemies are getting stronger
and stronger by the way, and we as
a country are getting weaker. Even
our nuclear arsenal doesn't work.

—Presidential bid announcement, June 16, 2015

*W*e need a leader that can bring back our
jobs, can bring back our manufacturing, can
bring back our military, can take care of our
vets. Our vets have been abandoned. And we
also need a cheerleader....We need somebody
that can take the brand of the United States
and make it great again. It's not great again.

—Presidential bid announcement, June 16, 2015

*S*adly, the American dream is dead. But if
I get elected president, I will bring it back
bigger and better and stronger than ever
before, and we will make America great again.

—Presidential bid announcement, June 16, 2015

I can never apologize for the truth.
I don't mind apologizing for things
but I can't apologize for the truth.

—Finance.yahoo.com, July 2, 2015

*T*he silent majority is back, and we're
going to take the country back.

—Speech at the Phoenix Convention Center,
Fox News Insider, July 12, 2015

I'm a Republican, I'm a conservative, I'm
in first place, I want to run as a Republican,
and I think I'll get the nomination.

—BBC, July 23, 2015

I think that I would be a great uniter. I think that I would have great diplomatic skills. I think that I would be able to get along with people very well. I've had a great success in my life. I think the world would unite if I were the leader of the United States.

—Interview with Jesse Byrnes, *The Hill*, July 30, 2015

*T*he fact is I give people what they need and deserve to hear—exactly what they don't get from politicians—and that is The Truth. Our country is a mess right now and we don't have time to pretend otherwise. We don't have time to waste on being politically correct.

—*Crippled America: How to Make America Great Again,*
by Donald J. Trump, 2015

$\mathcal{A}$ great leader has to be flexible, holding his ground on the major principles but finding room for compromises that can bring people together. A great leader has to be savvy at negotiations so we don't drown every bill in pork barrel bridges to nowhere. I know how to stand my ground—but I also know that Republicans and Democrats need to find common ground to stand on as well.

—*Crippled America: How to Make America Great Again,*
by Donald J. Trump, 2015

$\mathcal{I}$ know words. I have the best words.

—Speech in Hilton Head Island, South Carolina,
December 30, 2015

I'm very angry because our country is being run horribly and I will gladly accept the mantle of anger. Our military is a disaster. Our healthcare is a horror show.

—Transcript of the sixth Republican debate,
Charleston, South Carolina, January 14, 2016

*T*his is a movement. It is a movement going on. We want to take our country back. Our country is disappearing. You look at the kind of deals we make. You look at what's happening; our country is going in the wrong direction, and so wrong, and it's got to be stopped and it's got to be stopped fast.

—Speech at Liberty University, January 18, 2016

I'm the messenger, but I'll tell you what: the message is the right message.

—Speech at rally in Wilmington, North Carolina,
August 9, 2016

*T*o all the politicians, donors, and special interests, hear these words from me today: there is only one core issue in the immigration debate and it is this: the well-being of the American people.

—Immigration speech, Phoenix, Arizona, August 31, 2016

*N*o dream is too big; no challenge is too great. Nothing we want for our future is beyond our reach. America will no longer settle for anything less than the best.

—Victory speech after winning the 2016 presidential election, November 9, 2016

I was never a fan of the Electoral College until now

—*New York Times*, November 23, 2016

$\mathcal{W}$e the citizens of America are now joined in a great national effort to rebuild our country and restore its promise for all of our people. Together we will determine the course of America, and the world, for many, many years to come. We will face challenges. We will confront hardships, but we will get the job done.

— Inaugural address, January 20, 2017

$\mathcal{T}$he oath of office I take today is an oath of allegiance to all Americans...We assembled here today are issuing a new decree to be heard in every city, in every foreign capital, and in every hall of power. From this day forward, a new vision will govern our land. From this day forward, it's going to be only America first.

— Inaugural address, January 20, 2017

*W*hen you open your heart to patriotism, there is no room for prejudice. The Bible tells us how good and pleasant it is when God's people live together in unity. We must speak our minds openly, debate our disagreements, but always pursue solidarity. When America is united, America is totally unstoppable.

— Inaugural address, January 20, 2017

*F*inally, we must think big and dream even bigger. In America, we understand that a nation is only living as long as it is striving. We will no longer accept politicians who are all talk and no action, constantly complaining but never doing anything about it. The time for empty talk is over. Now arrives the hour of action. Do not allow anyone to tell you that it cannot be done. No challenge can match the heart and fight and spirit of America. We will not fail. Our country will thrive and prosper again.

—Inaugural address, January 20, 2017

The human soul yearns for discovery. By unlocking the mysteries of the universe, we unlock truths within ourselves. That's true. Our journey into space will not only make us stronger and more prosperous but will unite us behind grand ambitions and bring us all closer together. Wouldn't that be nice? Can you believe that space is going to do that? I thought politics would do that.

—While signing an executive order on the
National Space Council, June 30, 2017

I'm going to fight for every American in every last part of this nation.

—*Hardball with Chris Matthews*, August 4, 2017

*A*merica is governed by Americans.
We reject the ideology of globalism and
we embrace the doctrine of patriotism.

—Address to the UN General Assembly,
September 25, 2018

*S*ince the founding of our nation, many
of our greatest strides—from gaining
our independence, to abolition, [to]
civil rights, to extending the vote for
women—have been led by people of faith.

—Remarks, National Prayer Breakfast,
February 7, 2019

*T*he truth is plain to see—if you want freedom, take pride in your country; if you want democracy, hold on to your sovereignty; and if you want peace, love your nation.

—Address to United Nations General Assembly,
September 13, 2019

*W*e have an invisible enemy. We have a problem a month ago nobody ever thought about...This is a bad one, this is a very bad one. This is bad in the sense that it's so contagious. It's just so contagious—sort of record-setting–type contagion.

—Coronavirus Task Force press briefing,
March 16, 2020

*L*ook, I take responsibility always for everything because it's ultimately my job, too. I have to get everybody in line.

—Fox News, July 19, 2020

I know that everyone here will soon be marching over to the Capitol building to peacefully and patriotically make your voices heard.

—Save America rally speech, January 6, 2021

I am asking for everyone at the US Capitol to remain peaceful. No violence! Remember, WE are the party of Law and Order—respect the Law and our great men and women in Blue. Thank you!

—Twitter, January 6, 2021

$\mathcal{W}$e have just been through an intense
election and emotions are high. But now,
tempers must be cooled and calm restored.
We must get on with the business of America.

—Video on the U.S. Capitol breach, January 7, 2021

$\mathcal{N}$obody has done more for
Christianity or for evangelicals—or
for religion itself—than I have.

—*Newsweek*, October 2, 2021

$\mathcal{T}$he existence of evil in our world is not
a reason to disarm law-abiding citizens.
The existence of evil is one of the very
best reasons to arm law-abiding citizens.

—NRA convention speech, May 27, 2022

In order to make America great and glorious again, I tonight am announcing my candidacy for president of the United States.

—Candidacy speech, November 15, 2022

In 2016, I declared: I am your voice. Today, I add: I am your warrior. I am your justice. And for those who have been wronged and betrayed: I am your retribution...and I will put the people back in charge of this country again.

—CPAC keynote speech, March 4, 2023